Slots of Pain

By: Julie M. Barron

Dedication

I dedicate this book to all my fellow Gamblers Anonymous members. Without you I could never have quit my addiction. Listening to all of your stories and watching you come each week to our meeting has helped me keep the faith. This includes my sponsor, Michelle, who believed in me even though I gave her no reason to.

Contents

Forward

It's not easy admitting to yourself or to anyone else for that matter, that you are a compulsive gambler. I think it's even harder than admitting you have a mental illness. It has become socially acceptable for women to gamble. Our government urges us to gamble all in the name of education. But over the last two decades I've seen firsthand what gambling can do. I know what it has done to me and where I was headed. I hope that by telling my story that other women can see themselves clearer and hopefully help them to get off the path of self-destruction. It really can take it all from you, even your life. Please read these pages as a gift and may God be with you.

Chapter One –the Beginning

I'm doing it again - walking around the casino floor in a daze. I don't see anyone. I'm just staring ahead trying to think of some way of getting more money. I can't go home because I know that if I just had $20 more dollars I could hit a big jackpot and pay the bank back what I owe them now. I call this the Casino Zombie Walk. You see it a lot around 3 or 4 in the morning. It's not that people are tired. It's that they know that not only have they spent all the money they came in with but they are now in a financial hole. I can't tell you how many times I did this "walk". Then I would get in the car to go home and it would hit me. I'm going to have to borrow money from someone or somewhere. And then the anger starts. Why did I do this again? Why did I bang my head up against this wall again?

Gambling became my best friend, but it didn't start out that way. The first time I gambled was in 1976 when I went with my Dad, Mom, Aunt and Uncle to Las Vegas for a fun trip. You would think that a place like that for a gambler would be heaven, but I was actually disappointed with the experience. I got off the plane and there in the distance were the mountains. I was so disappointed that I couldn't see them up close. I wanted to touch them, but I just ended up walking the strip until my feet were swollen. I gambled my allotted money – so no problem there, but as I was young and naïve I wore a black tight skirt and black and white top with black hose and black high heels. I thought you were supposed to dress up to gamble there. The only thing I got was a guy sitting next to me acting like he thought I was a hooker. Luckily I had the good sense to get up and move away. My increasing disappointment continued with the special show I attended one evening with my parents and aunt and uncle. We went to a show where the women were nude from the waist up and it embarrassed me in front of my family. I was mortified. I wanted to crawl out from under the table and sneak out, but no…..I just sat there and pretended to enjoy the show. When we got up to leave, I couldn't get my shoes back on so I had to leave in my stocking feet. The slot machines weren't any fun either since they were just the reels; the video machines hadn't been invented yet. I thought gambling isn't all that great and just moved on from the experience, vowing I would never go back to Las Vegas again – and I never did. Too bad I didn't vow to never step in any casino again. That would have saved me a lot of grief, sorrow, money, bad reputation, closed bank accounts, bankruptcy, agony, damaged relationships, sleepless nights, and missed work.

Chapter Two – The real beginning

The second time I gambled was ten years later in 1986 when the Lottery started in Michigan. I bought a lotto ticket for $1.00 and won $100. I was so elated and I was hooked instantly! I thought this was the best thing that could ever happen to anyone and what a wonderful thing for the State to be giving citizens the opportunity to make money and for them to pay for education. This was my justification. Oh! How wrong I was then. Winning that $100 hooked me on lottery tickets for a long, long time. I didn't have a problem with buying them addictively for another decade and a half, but I know that's what hooked me eventually. At one point, I was buying $60 to $100 worth of lottery tickets at a time. I would buy them, go sit in the car and scratch them off. Or I would go home, scratch them off and then if I had any winners, I would immediately take them back to the store and buy some more and usually I would add $20 or$40 more. For a long time, even when I was in GA, I didn't think that Lottery Ticket buying was gambling. So I would lie every week and say I wasn't gambling even though I was buying Lottery tickets. It wasn't until after almost 8 years of doing this that I finally realized that the buying of the tickets kept me in the gambling frame of mind. So for the last year, I haven't bought one single ticket. I tried not buying them one time for 5 months but then went to the casino, so I told myself that it didn't matter if I bought them or not. But I know that is wrong. Not buying them keeps my thinking free of the gambling urge. It really does make a difference even though it seems so innocent. I remember that when I would buy the lottery tickets and lose it made me want to make up for it and then I would end up at the casino sooner or later. It's that urge and frame of mind that keeps you going and going.

I started going to casinos when the Indian Casinos first opened up in Michigan in the 80's. I had so many other things going on in my life like losing jobs and a mental illness so gambling became a getaway for me. My Mom and her friends and I would go on weekends up to Peshawbytown in Traverse City. They had a small building with about 8 machines. They had a picnic table outside where we would come early and play cards until they opened up at noon. We would each get a machine and stay on that machine until we were out of money. I only got to do this whenever I went to visit my Mom up north (upper Michigan) so it was only once a month or so or sometimes every 2 or 3 months. I never really spent a lot of money then because I didn't have a lot. But what I do remember is taking money from my Mom without ever paying it back. Little did I know that when my Dad died in 1992 my Mom would go on and spend all of the money that my Dad left her so she would eventually in 2000 have to sell her home. This was the house that my Dad designed and had built specifically for him and my Mom to retire in. I was devastated that she had to do this. My Mom didn't seem to be upset about it but I think she was more devastated then she let on. I think this might have been the reason she kept on gambling, to make up for the loss and to one day buy another home, which of course, never happened. I had feelings of regret over this but my gambling kept increasingly getting worse.

All through the 90's I and my mom and our friends would go with my mom to the Indian casinos and we would spend our money and then my mom would start handing out $100 bills to everyone. She would say – just pay me back when you win. Well no one ever won. This went on for ten years. I know that if my Dad were alive, my Mom would never have gone gambling that many times – he wouldn't have let her. I felt that I was partly responsible for my Mom losing her house. She had to sell it in 2000. Mom came to live with me in 2000 in a small apartment. The gambling got worse. We would go every other weekend and I would spend everything I had. I had been on disability in the 90's, but at that time I was off of disability and had just lost my full time job. I found another part-time job in Lansing. Quickly we went through the money that my Mom got from the sale of the house. I wasn't the only one but I sure was in the thick of it. Mom just didn't have a mind for money. My Dad had done all the money management all through their married life. It was foreign for my Mom to budget her money. She just went through it and ended up with no house and a monthly Social Security check. She didn't see it coming. She didn't know what hit her. I can't say that I was any better. I should have known better but I didn't. I too was use to my Dad managing my Mom's money. I wasn't any better at management of my own money. I had taken a loan out to finish my college degree. I graduated in 1998. I used half of my loan money to live on and yes you guessed it – to gamble with. I still owe a student loan and will probably have it for the rest of my life. Budgeting was not my strong suit. I am still struggling with it, but now without the gambling it is much easier.

Chapter Three – Complications

I have a mental illness. It has been a part of my life for 30 years. I believe my mental illness helped to intensify my gambling addiction. I would get depressed because I wasn't working and would go gambling to forget all the pain and anguish I was in. Then in 2001 I went to the casino with my Mom and I won $4,000 on a $1 poker machine. I was so elated. This solidified my gambling addiction and it went to a deeper more destructive level. The only thing my mental illness did was make it harder for me to quit gambling. The $4,000 was the most I had ever won. I remember they didn't take out the money for the taxes so I didn't pay the taxes on it. A couple of years later the IRS would come back after me for it. Then in 2002 I won the same amount of money in the same month – July – at the same casino at the same machines. I thought I was on this great winning streak. It was winning these jackpots that made my gambling intensify. It was then that I would go for 24-48 hours at a time. I started borrowing money from the Cash Advance places. At one time I had as many as 4 loans out at the same time. I started maxing out my credit card. I would spend $1,000 at a time and think I'll win to pay the bank back. But then the money would not be enough so I would have to borrow from family and friends to make it right with the bank. I had to close out my bank account and make a deal with the bank and a friend who loaned me $1,200 to pay the bank back. The rest of the money I owed I just set up a payment plan with the bank and eventually paid them back as well. But the bank closed out my account.

I started staying later and later at the casino. I wouldn't want to stop gambling even to go to the bathroom. I would ask the person next to me to watch my machine while I went to the bathroom. It even killed me to have to stop and go get something to eat. Because I was so sure that when I got back my machine would be cold. And of course the buffet was alluring. I would go sometimes just because I had points on my card and get a free meal. What a bargain! Yeah, do you think maybe the casinos do that on purpose? So many times when my mother was with me I would stay later and later. She would say that she was tired and wanted to go home, and I would be either telling her it will be soon or just ignoring her no matter how tired she was. One way I got her to stay later was giving her $20's every so often. I would say "Here go play with this" and she would be good for another hour. One time she even told me she was going to go sit in the car and I just ignored her. She went out to the car and just sat there for a couple of hours. I can't believe I treated my mother this way; it was so selfish and wrong and abusive! When you are gambling – nothing else matters. You don't care about anyone or anything, just putting in your next $20, because you just know that it's about to hit. The big win is just around the corner. That big elusive JACKPOT! I have heard of people winning thousands of dollars, even tens of thousands of dollars, and they always just put it right back in. And of course the casinos know this – that's why they can afford to offer these jackpots. They know it's just going right back into the machines. I started becoming like a zombie. I would spend everything I had and didn't have and then start walking around the casino in a daze knowing that I didn't have the money to pay the bank back. I would start loathing myself. On the way home it was worse. I would start getting angry. I would get so angry that I would start yelling and yelling. And guess who was in the car with me? My mom. She would hear the brunt of all my anger. I was angry at myself but she would hear it all. She would say that she was never going to another casino with me. But I would always talk her into it and she would forget all the anger and go with me. It's a funny thing. Not one of my friends was into casinos. They weren't even into the lottery. I only went once or twice with a friend. I went with my friend Judy because she said she wanted to see what it is that attracted me and she saw firsthand how I wouldn't want to go home. She told me afterwards that now she understood my addiction. She had not understood it before. I really miss my friend. She passed away last year. I know she would have been so proud of me with my clean time. She never got to see it.

What were the reasons I gambled? I gambled for lots of reasons.
I gambled out of boredom. I gambled to numb myself to my past.
I gambled for excitement. I gambled to forget my past. It didn't
take much to get me to want to go gambling either. I guess that's
why it was so hard for me to quit. The casinos know this. That's
the reason they have all the bells and whistles and lights. It really
is mesmerizing; not to mention the machines themselves. I
understand now that they actually hire psychologists to design
their machines. And can we not forget the substance used here.
Dopamine is released every time you get a jackpot, even the small
jackpots on these machines. That is how gambling is like all other
addictions.

I started writing checks on a balance that wasn't there. I didn't
know it but that is called kiting. I didn't know I was breaking the
law. By 2004 I was in over my head. I had alienated my Mother,
my sister, my brother-in law, and my brother. I had borrowed
money from all of them. I did pay them back but it got
ridiculous. I finally had to file for bankruptcy. It was then that I

first went to Gamblers Anonymous. It was a stroke of luck to find Gamblers Anonymous, but it would take another 8 years for me to stop gambling. This was my journey through a gambling addiction.

Some people find GA but they can quit right away, but it is an individual process for each person. The good part is that I eventually figured out what it was that I was doing wrong and what was holding me back from success. But I didn't do it alone – I had lots of help.

Chapter Four – Gamblers Anonymous

I notice one trend at my Gambler's Anonymous meetings over the years. Women don't tend to stay long; at least most of the women in my group. There are some who stay, but most get their year or two in and then quit. They either feel they have it down pat and don't need the group any more, or they go back to gambling. Then there are many of them who only stay for a short time and then go back out. I didn't fit this trend. I stayed in Gambler's anonymous for over 9 years, but I would slip and relapse every 2 or 3 months. Many people would just feel too embarrassed to come back or to keep coming back. I was embarrassed but my desire to quit was strong and something kept me coming back. It has taken 9 years for me to get one year of clean time. I also got myself into therapy at this time. In 2004 I tried to commit suicide and ended up in the hospital. This wasn't my first trip to the hospital and it wasn't the first time I had tried to commit suicide either. I had dabbled in self-destruction before when I was younger. I think this is a big reason that gambling had such an allure for me. It was an escape. It was a numbing out of all the bad feelings that I had pent up in me. You would think that I would know this, but it was the last thing on my mind. To me it was just fun. I didn't have to meet anyone – it was just me and the machines. It was slots of fun. But eventually I would learn that it was slots of pain as well. It was like hitting your head on a brick wall and then forgetting that you did it and come right back a month or two later and do it all over again. I would ask myself, "When are you going to learn?" It would take me another 8 years to find a sponsor, and when I did things began to change.

Chapter Five – Slots of Pain –

What was my preference in the casino? It was any new slot machine, but basically I played them all – new and old. I had a fondness for the old machines too.   They called us Slot Sluts. And that's what I was basically. I would get on a machine and stay there whether I was winning or losing, thinking that eventually this thing is going to hit. Most of the time, though, the machines only took my money and once in a while it would give back a little. Besides the poker machine wins the most I won was $1,000 on a slot machine. I loved Cleopatra and the Bear and the fish.   I would make the rounds and eventually end up playing more time at the ATM machine. When my money ran out at the ATM then I would do the floating of the checks. When I went into bankruptcy my lawyer told me that one of the Indian casinos told him that I owed them $200 and they were going to tell the authorities if I didn't pay them back. My lawyer set up a payment plan and I paid them back. I didn't realize that what I was doing was breaking the law. This never occurred to me.

When I did the 20 questions in GA I did not tell them that I broke the law to feed my gambling addiction. It wasn't until years later that I realized what I had done. The gambling took a lot from me. Time from my family and friends except those times I was with my mother gambling. But even when I was with her on the gaming floor, we weren't really together. I would be on my machine and she would be somewhere on hers. The only time we hooked up was when one of us was out of money or wanted to go home. We seldom sat next to each other and talked although we did once in a while. But even those times I wouldn't be more engrossed in what was happening on the screen than what my mother was saying or doing. I know I have one regret that I will never forget. All those weekends that I spent at the casino, my cat Dickens was left at home in the dark all alone. When I lost him to cancer when he was 13, I regretted all those times I left him alone. So now with my new cat Phoenix, I am so very aware that I don't leave him alone except when I have to go out of town for work. I want to make it up to Phoenix and I do.

Chapter Six – Lies and consequences –

What were some of the other consequences of gambling? There were many. It's funny how you don't forget these things. I remember one time my mom and I were with my sister and a few friends and we went to the Upper Peninsula to gamble. While we were in there it started snowing – real heavy! By the time we left the casino, there were white out conditions. At one point I started to go over an overpass and hit a patch of black ice. The car immediately started to swerve out of control. To keep control, I pulled off the road on to the meridian. I think I bent the wheel rim but we stopped. A highway patrolman stopped by and asked me if I had trouble driving. I told him no – it is the black ice on the overpass and to get ready cause there's going to be more cars. He turned around and sure enough 3 more cars ran off the road. I somehow got the car back onto the freeway and started driving, but one of my Mom's friends said that if we didn't stop at a motel right now she was going to have a heart attack. So I stopped at the next exit and we stayed at a cheap motel for the night. The next morning we got back home and I had to get the car fixed. So I asked myself – "Is this worth it?". The answer was "no" but still I continued to gamble for years. It's like – what does it take? Another time my Mom and I (the dynamic duo) went to an Indian casino on the west side of the state. We left the casino in the wee hours of the night. Suddenly my Mom says she has a charlie horse in her leg. I had to stop at a gas station and we had to walk around until the pain went away. By the time we got to Grand Rapids I was out of gas. I pulled into a gas station and suddenly realized that neither of us had any money and we didn't have any credit cards either – Mom had maxed hers out and I couldn't get one. I went into the gas station and told the attendant my problem. He said "I'm sorry mam I can't do anything." A guy was standing nearby and called me over and said here take this. He gave me $5.00 which in those days was enough to get home with. I told him to give me his address and I would mail him the $5 back and he just said forget it. He said I would want someone to do that for me. We made it home. You would think that this would be enough to get me to stop gambling – but "NO" I continued for years after. OK w... take?

I remember many times coming home around 3 or 4 am or 6 or 7 am in the morning and having to stop at the rest stop and sleep. I just couldn't keep my eyes open. It's really a major wonder how I ever got home without an accident or two or three. I was soooo lucky that I didn't hit a deer. That was just amazing to me. And the sad part of it is that I'm not the only one. There are many people today that do this kind of reckless driving home from casinos every day. I'm sure there are some horror stories out there. I guess God watches over stupid people too.

I ask myself why gambling is an addiction. I found one answer. *How can a person be addicted to something that isn't a substance?* "Although no substance is ingested, the problem gambler gets the same effect from gambling as someone else might get from taking a tranquilizer or having a drink. The gambling alters the person's mood and the gambler keeps repeating the behavior attempting to achieve that same effect. But just as tolerance develops to drugs or alcohol, the gambler finds that it takes more and more of the gambling experience to achieve the same emotional effect as before. This creates an increased craving for the activity and the gambler finds they have less and less ability to resist as the craving grows in intensity and frequency."

Ok so this makes sense to me. I no longer ask myself why I don't have the willpower to stop gambling. There is no such thing as willpower when gambling. It is an addiction and I need to keep reminding myself of that. So many judges do not see this when they get people before them who have committed a crime trying to feed their addiction. That is something that needs to change.

Chapter Seven – Not another relapse?

I was actually in counseling on and off since the 80's but I never clicked with anyone and I didn't see gambling as a problem until after 2003. When I went to CEI-CMH in Lansing I was paired with a counselor who just got it. She understood and she believed my story, which a lot of counselors didn't. She supported my decision to go to Gambler's anonymous. So I was seeing her every week and going to GA every week. I would relapse every couple of weeks or months. But for some reason I didn't quit GA. I would come even though in the beginning there was this guy who would give me grief about it. One day he just yelled at me and said I shouldn't come in here like a dog with its tail between its legs. Lucky for me I lasted longer than he did. He finally went to another county and most of the people in our group were glad of that fact. Most of the people at GA were very understanding. They had to be since I would continue to come even though I would slip every few months. I can't tell you how many 30 day key chains I received and how many 90 day key

I collected. There were too many to count. I would just give them back so they wouldn't have to buy new ones all the time. But people never said anything to me. They just quietly accepted me and supported me and they were there for me. I don't pretend that because I have a year in of continuous clean time that I have it all sown up. No it is far from it. I still have urges. And it seems that one of the medications that I'm taking for my depression may actually be contributing to my urges. I wondered why my urges were becoming more intense lately and it seems to have happened right about the same time I started taking Wellbutrin. My therapist told me that Wellbutrin acts by increasing dopamine. Hooya! Isn't that the chemical that reacts when you get a hit on a slot machine? As a matter of fact yes it is. Good ole' Dopamine - the chemical that casinos count on to keep people playing by offering occasional small hits.[1i] So you would think that now I know that my medication is causing me to have more intense urges that I would just tell my doctor and she will put me on another anti-depressant. Simple - right? Not really.

[1] Stein DJ, Grant JE. Betting on dopamine. CNS Spectrums 2005; 10:88-90.

Wellbutrin is the 4th anti-depressant that I've tried. I won't go back to Paxil because of its side effects like weight gain to name just one. She tried SSRI's on me and it turns out I'm allergic to them. I get hives. So Wellbutrin is a drug of last resort. I had a choice. I've decided that for now I would deal with the urges. I feel I have enough clean time in that my coping mechanisms are better and chances are that I will be able to fight the urges. But after a while I had side effects from that as well so I stopped taking it and the urges went away. I do other things to take care of my depression. Counseling is one of them. Getting exercise is another. There are many things you can do to feel better.

I want to say something about internet gambling here. I have never played internet gaming for money. But I have played the FREE slot games on the internet. These games are there to make money, so even though you are playing for free, they often ask you to pay $5 or $1 for more coins. It is very enticing. I don't play these games anymore because they can trigger urges. One of the reasons these games are there is to make people want to go to the casino. I wouldn't be surprised if the casinos are funding some of these sites. I use to play these games when I had internet at home. I would play them for hours into the wee hours of the night. Then the next day or week I'd be at the casino. It seems harmless enough but the games are so similar to real slot machines that the same urges pop up. When I got rid of my internet at home because I was saving money, I started going to the library and getting on Facebook. Facebook is riddled with the advertisements of slot games. All you have to do is click on them and you are routed to those sites. You can play for free, but the chances of getting an urge to do some "Real" gambling is there. I highly recommend that you don't play these games. Even though you can do them "Free" they still constitute gambling. There are games that I allow myself to play, such as solitaire that comes with my computer. I would play games like scrabble also. These are more everyday games that don't resemble slot machines. It seems like it's being picky not being able to play these free slot games but it really can sabotage even the best of intentions, and I stay away from them.

Let me just say one more thing about relapses. I feel as though I just now, with one year clean time in, have gotten the message. It is Day One for me. I am starting on a journey that took me 9 years to begin. That seems like a really long time to get something and it is. It's like a stubborn donkey who refuses to go forward. I just hung on with dear might being afraid to let go. But letting go is not giving up like I felt it was. Letting go is letting the freedom begin. It is letting God take over – or my High Power take over. It's not me white knuckling it to be in control any more. It takes some sense of trust to do that. I trust in my GA group, my sponsor, my friends who don't gamble, and my Higher Power. Yes I trust myself too but not exclusively any more. It's really is freeing.

Chapter Eight All In the family

Some of my family may never really get my addiction, but at least with more clean time I put in the more they will see that I am serious about quitting. Just the other day, my sister sent me a chain letter with a $1 lottery ticket in it. I thought "What does it take for you to get it?" I sent it back with a note inside telling her that I was in GA and I don't gamble. I have to say though that I don't blame her for thinking that I would play this game. How many years have I been trying to quit gambling? It's been 9 years. No wonder she thinks I would buy some tickets. I bought tickets many times during the 8 years I was trying to quit. I haven't bought them in the past year, but she didn't know that. Many people don't see the buying of lottery tickets as gambling. They just don't connect it to real gambling especially since the State sponsors it. Why on earth would the government sponsor gambling? But they do. Some day my Mom will stop asking me to go with her to the casino and stop telling me that all I have to do is keep my credit card and check book at home. Little does she know that you don't even need a checkbook at the casino for them to get into your checking account. It is just soooooo easy to spend money there.

It is really hard for people who don't have a gambling addiction or any addiction for that matter to understand it. I had recently a conversation with my youngest sister on the phone. It went something like this:

Me: "Hi, do you want to go to a movie today?"

Sister: "We just went yesterday. I think you're addicted to movies. I think it's just as bad as your gambling addiction."

Me: "I don't think so, I go to movies sometimes when I have a gambling urge."

Sister: "No you have an addiction to movies."

I stopped the conversation there. I talked with my gambling therapist and she said that my sister was wrong on so many levels. To illustrate this point let me make a comparison of the two activities.

Movies: Miles to get there from my home: 34 miles round trip each time; Time spent in activity: 4 hours total for two movies; Cost: for two movies on a weekend: <$40.00. (this includes pop and popcorn.)

Gambling at casino: Miles to get to casino round trip >160 miles; Time spent in activity: 8-48 hours depending on how long my money lasts;

Cost: $300-$1,000 or emptying of check book, maxing of credit card and then writing of floating checks when money runs out - then borrowing from cash advance the next day to cover gambling and/or borrowing of money from friends or family to cover debt. And then there's the depression and anger afterwards. There just is no comparison between the two. I go to movies to help with my urges and it is a fairly low cost way to do it. True $40.00 can add up, but I don't have urges to go to the movie during the week and often I don't go when there is no movie I want to see.

My sister has either never been in a casino or maybe she went one

has no clue what I do when I'm there and she has no

what an addiction truly is.

Even though I have a year of clean time in that doesn't mean my urges have stopped. I've been told that I could still have urges for up to five years. So I'm in it for the long haul. I can't let my guard down. I know that when my other sisters and my mother go to the casino, that it will create within me an urge to go myself. I still feel the pangs of jealousy that they can go and not have a problem and I can't. But I keep the past experiences in my mind. I also keep the prize in front of me. What is that prize? It is freedom from worry and the chance of losing it all. I don't want to lose my job. I don't want to lose my bank account. I don't want to lose my clean time. I don't want to lose the reputation I've built up. It's just too much to lose. I want that clear head and freedom from worry and doubt. I want the chance to find other dreams worth working toward.

Chapter Nine – A Real Lucky Break

In 2006 I was urged by my counselor to apply for a job at the CMH I was getting services at. I couldn't believe it but they had a job that the prerequisite was that you had to be getting services to apply – you had to be in recovery from a mental illness. This boggled my mind. You mean to tell me that my mental illness has a bright side. There is something good about it? Are you trying to tell me that you can recover from a mental illness? So I applied for the Customer Services Representative job and got it! It was suppose to be part time, but I asked my future boss if I could go full time and she said yes! I was just so sick of being on disability. I was ready to take the plunge. I got lots of training which not only helped me do my job and help others, but helped me at the same time. I learned how to recover and to handle my mental illness. I took classes on WRAP (Wellness Recovery Action Plan) by Mary Ellen Copeland, and PATH (Personal Action towards Health) by Stanford University. I took Money Smart which helped me to help others budget money more wisely. I took Mental Health First Aid which is a 12 hour course from the National Behavioral Health Council, to help people see the warning signs of mental illness and to help people to get into professional help. I also showed movies for free to the clients and we had Creative Recovery classes – like painting, crafts and writing classes. I also took a Recovery Coach training. The problem with that was that you had to have at least one year of clean time to be able to help others. So I took the training but wasn't able to use the training, until now.

Each and every one of the classes that I trained for not only helped me to help others with their recovery, but it helped me with mine. At one time I didn't even think that Recovery was possible. I thought like many people that once you had a mental illness or an addiction, that was it – you had it for life without ever being able to do anything about it let alone fulfill your dreams.

Lucky for me I continued to attend GA because I think

the biggest reason why I didn't lose my job. Yes ther

that I didn't come in on a Monday because I was gambling that

weekend before because of a relapse. But it was only a few times.

One thing I did which I am really glad and proud of was to tell

my boss about my addiction. I wanted her to be aware of what I

was up against. She already knew I had a mental illness, but now

she knew I also had an addiction. I wanted to be accountable. It

was much better that she knew because I would really make an

attempt to be in on time and not miss any time from work due to

my gambling. She was really supportive and she didn't get angry

or act disappointed.

Somewhere around 2010, I went to a gambling counselor. He was

helpful, but I wasn't ready to quit. He had me do a lot of

exercises and write some goals that I had but still I would slip

every couple of months. I went the allotted 16 weeks with him

twice in two years time. The state of Michigan has the NSO

(Neighborhood Service Organization) which allows you to get 16 weeks of free or very low cost gambling counseling. The regular casinos in the state help to fund this, which is the only thing I think that the casinos get right. I still didn't stay away from the casinos. Then he suggested I go to another gambling counselor who just happened to be a woman. She really got that for woman gambling is different than for men. She understood me and I am still going to her. We go over the steps when I get done writing them. She also lent me a couple of books written by women about gambling that were very helpful. She has given me several workbooks to read and work in that have been extremely helpful in understanding my addiction. It's important to know that women are more drawn to slot machines than men, although men play them too. Many women are escape gamblers and slot machines really fit the bill. Many woman talk about being drawn into the slot machine as if they are living the action themselves. I know that I would become mesmerized by the action on the screen and could tune out everything and everybody else around me. And I would do this for hours without stopping. People talk of 'casino time' where you lose the track of time. If you nc there are no clocks in the casino. And usually there are no windows especially in and around the gaming floor. I would lose track of time and could stay "in action" for hours not to mention sometimes days.

Finally in 2012 I met a woman in our GA group who had 5 years clean time in. She came from Chicago. She went up to me after the meeting and asked if I would like her to be my sponsor. I thought this was great since I had never had a sponsor before. There just weren't enough women in our group who had enough clean time. She started me on working the Twelve Steps of Recovery of Gamblers Anonymous, something that I hadn't done ever before. So I started writing and writing and writing. I am currently on step 4 but it seems to be helping. One thing I was supposed to do with my sponsor was bring my writing to her after each step and we would go over it. Well that never happened because she became ill. I mean big time ill. She went to the hospital and found out she had 3 autoimmune diseases. So she suggested to me that I bring my writing to my gambling therapist. Every couple of weeks I take what I've written and go over it with her. I really get to delve into why I gamble, why it is so hard to stop and what is really bugging me. When I finish one step, my sponsor will send me the next step. Each step has several questions that I'm to answer and it really gets me thinking. Like I would never have thought to even think about how I view my Higher Power. I didn't realize that the reason I don't go to church any more is that I don't have the same beliefs that I did growing up. I still believe in a Higher Power but that Higher Power is different. It's not that I don't believe in Christian principles anymore, I just don't believe in organized religion for myself. I don't even mention it to my mother as she would be really upset with me knowing this. I guess my beliefs are ever changing. Sometimes I feel that my spirituality is getting stronger with each step I take. I read from the "One Day at a Time" book every day. I read anything I can get on gambling and also spirituality and God. Maybe one day I will return to church but right now the praying, reading and meditation are enough.

There is another aspect to consider about my gambling. It is a known fact that 90% of people who have a mental illness have had some sort of Trauma in their lives. I wouldn't doubt that this also applies to compulsive gamblers. I had plenty of traumas in my life especially around my 30's and 40's. I had two sexual assaults and I lost countless jobs which in and of itself is a trauma. I know that I gambled often because I wanted to numb out all the past feelings that I had. I wouldn't doubt that other people who have a problem with gambling are trying to numb out also. Trauma can take many forms. It could be a divorce - especially ugly ones, losing someone. I know I was traumatized when my Dad died in 1992. It could be car accidents, I had that too. It could come from flunking out of school - I did that twice before I finally finished my degree. Trauma can take many forms. I learned from a woman who had both a mental illness and an addiction that trauma needs to be addressed. She wrote a book called "Trauma and the Twelve Steps". I have her listed in my resource page. She goes all over the country and basically tells people that you have to consider trauma when dealing with people who have mental illness and/or addictions. You can't just say - Oh, well, they're just an addict - so treat that. You have to know what their past has been. Some people may not agree with that, but I've found it to be so true in my life. My therapist is dealing with my addiction and my past trauma. Have you ever stopped to think of what trauma 9-11 caused people, not just those immediately involved, such as the families of the victims and the responders, but also of people in this country who felt violated? I know it really affected me. I know that part of that was from the depression that I was fighting. After 9-11, I packed up a suitcase and packed up all of my stuffed animals and without telling my family I headed for New York. I only took $40 with me and had no idea how to get to New York. I got as far as Pennsylvania and ended up at a hospital, where I walked in and took all my stuffed animals to the Pediatrics ward. Afterward, I sat in the car and contemplated suicide. I couldn't decide how to do it so I continued on. When dark came I ended up in the parking lot of a Catholic church. I slept there overnight and in the morning I went to church because it was Sunday. I attended church and afterward went up to the priest and asked if I could use his phone. I called a friend of the family in Connecticut and told her where I was at. She told me to come there and gave me directions. I headed to New York and for a moment while I was at the toll booth I thought about turning off and going to the scene but I couldn't figure out how to do that so I headed for Connecticut. I met my friend at a fast food place and followed her to her house. I stayed with her for a few days and then headed home. My family was relieved when I came home and really didn't understand my actions. Trauma really does affect us more than we think. You need to take this into consideration when trying to figure out why you gamble and what to do to stop it.

Chapter Ten – Another story

Here is a story from my sponsor – Michelle:

I entered the GA rooms on June 9, 2008. I had been accused of embezzlement by my former employer and in the process lost my family, friends, and career. I was "broken" and on the brink of suicide. I could not believe what 14 years of progressively worse compulsive gambling had brought my life to. I was just 35 years old and could not imagine what my future could be. Everyone who was at my first GA meeting describes me as a distraught woman staring straight down. My shame engulfed me and I could barely get a word out of my therapy before breaking into tears. I was looking at the possibility of legal consequences and could only imagine being handcuffed and brought to jail at any minute based on my former employers accusations.

I cannot say that walking into the GA rooms at first was easy. However, having lost most of everything, it was the only place I belonged. I attended three meetings my first week and eight meetings my second week. I started to recognize people. I started to listen to other people's stories. Suddenly I realized, I had done nothing different from anyone else. Addiction is an emotional illness and if I wanted to get help, I needed to keep coming to GA and also to get the counseling necessary to understand why I had turned to addiction. So, I kept attending GA meetings. I started going to counseling at a gambling outpatient facility. I worked my steps with my sponsor. I started to lift my head a little.

Fast forward one year and I started a new GA meeting, was an intergroup representative, and became social chair for the regional intergroup. GA became a place of friends, community, understanding, and support. My life started to turn around as well. I was hired into a better job than the one I was terminated from. I started to consider going back to school to earn a new graduate degree. I was surrounded by family and new friends. I was not gambling. Recovery saved my life, literally.

I am now nearly five years in recovery. Through that time, I have given back a lot to the GA program. However, I could never give GA back what it gave me. It gave me "One Day at a Time" and so many other things that make my life better than ever prior to recovery. Even my worst days now are better than my best days when I was lost in addiction. The legal consequences of my past actions came to fruition and I continue to face them with a community of support and my head held high. I do not worry about what is to come. I live for my recovery and for those things I love. Prior to entering GA I felt so alone – even when I was surrounded by others. Now, I never feel alone and I know I will always be supported and loved. I hope in my own small way, I am able to pay forward the gifts that the GA program and the people within the rooms have given to me.

Chapter Eleven – What seems to work

There are many stories out there of women who lost almost everything due to their gambling. It is becoming more and more common. I hope these things will help you if you are dealing with an addiction of gambling. Some of the things I did to finally get my gambling under control were to:

1. Keep going to GA, even if you relapse – keep coming back!

2. See a gambling counselor that I could relate to – in my case it was a woman counselor,

3. Find a sponsor who had some significant clean time in, and

4. Work the steps – not just read them but to actually WORK the steps with lots of writing.

5. I also made sure I wasn't buying lottery tickets on the side. That was a major stumbling block for me for so many years.

6. Another thing I did was to tell everyone I knew that I was a compulsive gambler including my boss. It really helps with accountability.

7. <u>Use the phone list from GA</u>. Talking to other people when you get the urge to gamble is extremely helpful especially when they have been there and know what you are going through.

It is really important to have some healthy activities to take the place of your gambling time. Without developing these activities, the risk of going back to gambling is high. Some of the things that I did to keep myself occupied and happy were:

1. As I indicated before I went to a lot of movies. This occupied many nights that I had usually reserved for gambling.

2. I took up knitting again. My family is inundated with my dishcloths.

3. Exercise: I bought a bike and in the spring, summer and fall I will go out biking around town. Exercise is a really good way to subdue the urges too! If you get an urge, a good 15 minute walk will usually get rid of them. Swimming is also a good calming exercise.

4. I really got into card-making which helps for birthdays and Christmas time.

5. Writing: I write in my journal about the 12 steps and share it with my counselor; writing this book itself was a great help. Telling your story is a good way to combat the urge to gamble. Everyone has a story to tell. I also like to write children's stories and poetry. Poetry is a good way to get out the feelings that gambling keeps pent up inside.

6. Reading: this usually keeps your mind occupied and you can learn a lot of things like history and about gambling. It is also very entertaining.

7. I took a watercolor painting class and now when I'm really bored I can take out my paints and usually entertain myself for a few hours. This is also good for calming those urges.

8. Listening to music is very helpful. Going to concerts is a good way to use up the time that usually was reserved for gambling. Having something planned for those days that you usually gambled – like Friday and Saturday nights – is of great help.

9. There are so many things you can do to keep your life interesting, like taking up a hobby or traveling and visiting friends and family and seeing new places - as long as it's not to a casino.

For those of you who just don't want to quit gambling, I need to tell you that it doesn't get better by itself. Things will just keep happening and unfortunately they keep getting worse. There is a guy by the name of Mike in my GA group that went to prison for 3 years for embezzlement because of his gambling. He wrote a book called "Never Enough". In his book he says that you never can win enough money to cover your losses and when you do win big, you either put it back and you keep gambling because it's never enough. There's another person in my GA group, Bernie, who wrote a book about his gambling addiction of lottery tickets. It really can take over your life just like slots or any other form of gambling. For me slot machines were my lover, my best friend, my addiction. I finally feel away from it enough to know that there is more to life than chasing that unattainable dream. There are other dreams out there that are there for the taking if only my head is clear enough to see them. There are people out there that will help you find your dreams and attain them. The people in my GA group really get it. They understand the lure, they understand the compulsion. They are there for me every week and whenever I need one of them – they are on the phone list. It is because of their clean time that I kept my dream alive. I keep this phone list with me at all times.

Chapter Twelve – Some statistics to ponder

Here are some ways to know if you have a gambling problem:

- A preoccupation with gambling, either by reliving past gambling, planning for future gambling experiences, and/or thinking of ways to secure money to finance gambling

- Needing more and more money for gambling in order to achieve the desired level of gambling enjoyment

- Repeated unsuccessful attempts to stop or reduce betting behaviors

- Becoming uneasy or easily irritated when trying to reduce or stop gambling

- Gambling for the purpose of escaping problems or to relieve sadness or anxiety

- Returning to gambling after losing money in an effort to recoup losses

- Lying to family or other loved ones, mental-health professionals, or others in an effort to hide the extent of the gambling behavior

- Committing crimes (for example, stealing, fraud, or forgery) in an effort to finance gambling

- Risking important relationships, employment, or other opportunities due to gambling

- Depending on others for money to resolve dire financial situations that are the result of gambling.

What are some of the side effects of gambling? As much as $5 billion is spent on gambling in the United States every year, with people who are addicted to gambling accruing tens to hundreds of thousands of dollars in debt. Harmful effects that compulsive gambling can have on the individual include financial problems ranging from high debt, bankruptcy or poverty, to legal problems resulting from theft to prostitution, to wanting, attempting or completing suicide.

Chapter Thirteen – The Hope Factor

Even though I don't understand my Higher Power, I know He is there for me. I guess He watches over me more than I realize. There were so many times when I could have really hurt myself or lost more than I did. I could have lost my job and that would have been devastating. The job I have now is the longest I have ever stayed at one job. I used to have a new job every year or two. I have been at this job for 7 years now. My recovery from mental illness and my addiction are the reasons I have kept my job this long. If you would have told me that one day I would keep a job for as long as 7 years, I would have said you were nuts. I went for 30 years going from job to job. It is a testament to my group in GA, my sponsor and my determination and my recovery that I've managed so far. My GA group gave me hope. I know that without hope I wouldn't have made it. I would have not only relapsed but stayed out and continued to gamble and who knows where that would have lead me.

I kept going to GA and that was a big reason why. I am now able to say – "I get it!" I hope you will be able to say that someday too. And remember – "Never give up!" You need to keep hope in sight. The Serenity Prayer really says it all. "God Grant me the Serenity to accept the things I cannot change. Courage to change the things I can and Wisdom to know the difference. "And may I add "Hope to dream". I've been told by GA'ers that courage doesn't mean without fear, it means doing it anyway and succeeding. I hope now that I know the difference between a mirage and a real dream. Dreams are something we need to aspire to. And dreaming of that big win isn't going to do it for you because it is so illusory. Here is a poem I put together while riding in to work:

A Dragon called Addiction

Crumbling, crumbling
There goes my addiction
You thought because I was a woman
That you could easily defeat me.
But I know where your soft unprotected underbelly lies....
I have a whole arsenal at my disposal.
I was under your spell
For oh so long,
But now I have slain you!

You may still come back to life someday
But I'll be ready for you....
Your fire breathing sting has gone out
In a puff of smoke.
I have my life back
The Dragon called Addiction
Is now a lizard basking in the sun
Waiting for me to slumber.
But I am ready for you...
Freedom reigns!

And for all the women who, like me, have fought to keep their lives together against all the odds. I offer this poem that I wrote in 1994. It was originally for a woman who fought the battle of mental illness but it also reminds me of all the women who fight the addiction of gambling like me:

A Woman

I know a friend
>   *Who's seen more than you or I*
>   >   *Walked a longer mile*
>   >   *Talked a harder fight*
>   >   *Cried a larger tear . . .*
>   *Just to live through the night.*

I know a person
>   *Who's born more pain*
>   *Than a town full of people yet she*
>   >   *Smiled a sweeter smile*
>   >   *Hugged a tighter hug*
>   >   *Sang a softer song*
>   >   *Loved with all her might*

I know a person
>   *Who could have failed like so many*
>   *But she . . .*
>   >   *Stood a head taller*
>   >   *Climbed a higher mountain*
>   >   *Sailed a more distant star*
And she won the right
To be called a Woman.

Julie Barron 1994

RESOURCES:

Gambling Hotline: (800-270-7117)

Gam-Anon International Service Office, Inc. (For family members of gamblers.)
P.O. Box 157
Whitestone, NY 11357
718-352-1671

Gamblers Anonymous (GA) International Service Office
P.O. Box 17173
Los Angeles, CA 90017
213-386-8789
isomain@gamblersanonymous.org

Problem Gambling.com
24 Hours a Day
7 Days a Week
U.S. Gambling Hotline: 1-800-522-4700
Canadian Gambling Hotline: 1-888-391-1111

Jamie Marich, Ph.D., "Trauma and the Twelve Steps", website:
www.TraumaTwelve.com

Bio:

I have 5 younger brothers and sisters, their husbands and wives and 12 nieces and nephews and 3 great nieces. I live with my cat Phoenix. I love to write, read, knit and walk and bike and go to movies. I've lived in Michigan all of my life except for 5 years in Ohio.

———————————————